Write to Riches Journal

Freewriting to Tap into Your Genius

Write to Riches

Renee Rose

Copyright © October 2022 Write to Riches Journal by Renee Rose and Renee Rose Romance

All rights reserved. This copy is intended for the original purchaser of this book ONLY. No part of this book may be reproduced, scanned, or distributed in any printed or electronic form without prior written permission from the authors. Please do not participate in or encourage piracy of copyrighted materials in violation of the authors' rights. Purchase only authorized editions.

Published in the United States of America

Wilrose Dream Ventures LLC

Cover image by Jade Beall Photography

Cover Design by Kismet Covers

❀ Created with Vellum

Want Author Affirmations Sent to Your Inbox?

Author Abundance Affirmations

Sign up to receive a weekly Millionaire Author Affirmation delivered straight from the Universe (via me) to your inbox! These weekly reminders will keep you on track and positive as you become your Millionaire Author self. https://www.subscribepage.com/authorabundanceaffirmations

About this Workbook

This workbook is a companion guide to *Write to Riches: 7 Practical Steps to Manifesting Abundance from Your Books.* Abundance mindset can and will change your life. Mindset is everything. It takes away the ache of feeling like what you want is out of reach. It soothes the wounds inflicted by comparisons and perceived failures. It eases the tension and anxiety produced by the belief that you'll get there if you just try harder. Or finally get it right.

There is no right.

You are already perfect.

And you can have it all.

If you follow the seven steps in the book–not as a one-and-done, linear attempt but as a practice–you will manifest all your desires. I can't say when or how. All I know is that the more you believe in yourself–your magic, your potential, your power–the more powerful you become.

The book was designed to light the flame of abundance mentality for you, so you will be open to having the right answers, the right connections, all the magic of the Universe drop into your lap at the right time. When you believe in yourself and your books, when you're open to receiving abundance, that's when the quantum entanglements can work to propel your career to the highest heights.

You will no longer be creating by default—functioning from old operating systems rooted in fear or lack of self-worth. You can now create with intention. Envision the career you want for yourself, invite the energy of that future into your now.

I believe you can achieve all your targets as an author without pushing yourself. You can ask the Universe to assist you and receive that assistance with total ease. You can allow the Universe to deliver in ways you can't even contemplate yet, but you follow your inner guidance, take action when you know you are supposed to, write what you love, market it from the heart, and let the Universe work all its magic to keep you in abundance.

I know you can achieve this vision you have for yourself.

Remember that there are no mistakes—every choice you make will move you forward.

You've got it, and we're here for you. You can harness the magic of the Universe to create this for yourself.

Join the Community

One of the best ways to see abundance in your life is to surround yourself with like-minded people. It's said that energetically, we are the average of the five people we're around every day, so we want to make sure those people are who we wish to be like.

If you're ready to surround yourself with other authors dwelling in possibilities and interested in uplifting others, we invite you to join us in our Author Abundance Central Facebook. https://www.facebook.com/groups/authorabundance/

Sign up to receive Author Abundance Affirmations sent straight to your inbox every week! https://www.subscribepage.com/authorabundanceaffirmations

Write to Riches Journal

Join the Author Abundance monthly membership for live coaching, energetic clearing, meditation, and discussion of what's possible. https://millionaire-author-coaching.teachable.com/p/author-abundance-membership

How to Use the Workbook

Where to start

This workbook follows the order of the seven steps from *Write to Riches*, but you don't have to fill it in or follow in that order.

You may choose to use your workbook more like a tarot deck—holding it in your hands and setting your intention to open to the prompt or section that has exactly what you need that day, then seeing what page the journal opens on.

I suggest journaling first thing in the morning when your subconscious is still fresh, but any time you're called to it is perfect.

You don't have to fill all the lines allotted. If you find there isn't enough room to write, feel free to use the additional sheets at the back, add notebook paper, or continue in your own journal.

About Freewriting

When you approach the journal contemplations, treat them like you would a freewriting exercise. Shut off the internal editor. Don't think—just write. You're going to tap into your subconscious or intuition to get the answers that will truly contribute to your abundance and the future you're trying to create. You're contemplating in writing—everything is unpacking—every thought, every impulse, every feeling, every picture that comes to you. Allow it all. Begin with the first thing that comes to mind. Don't try to get the right answer or to answer from your cognitive brain—conclusions limit possibilities. Instead, really use your perception and awareness to access your contemplations and allow them space on the page and in your consciousness.

Remember—keep the pen moving across the page. This is the place of allowing, of freedom, of courage. This isn't the place to edit. Allow the ideas to flow, so you can tap into your subconscious and really dig into the intuitive answers that will bring you maximum insight. The more you allow yourself to play with your contemplations, the faster you can clear all your blocks to abundance. Are you willing to surprise yourself?

Write until nothing more comes out, then move onto the next one. If you get tired or feel exhausted, take a break and come back to it later. This isn't a race. You're moving to a life in which you truly embody and live abundance. Where riches are your easy norm. When you truly allow yourself to fully explore, it can be a lot for your nervous system to absorb. You're bringing the anti-consciousness—the knowledge you are resisting in your life—into consciousness. There are things we stick our heads in the sand about—this will uncover them. Your entire construct of reality may shatter and fall, and that's okay. That's what we want. After all, what are you letting go of? Lack. Limits. Beliefs that trap you. You have to be willing to leave behind the old to become the new. Are you ready to learn something new about yourself? Are you ready to truly explore? To see everything?

The great thing about these contemplations is that you can return to them. You might be willing to allow some aspect of a belief into your consciousness, and later, when you contemplate again, something else emerges. Clearing limiting beliefs is not a one-and-done process. With each layer of the onion we allow ourselves to pull back, we get to the truth of who we are, and from that expanded place, we can dive in again and again, continually receiving.

Clear the Deck

In this first step, we dig into all the blockages, limiting beliefs and core wounds that drag your energetic field down and keep you from being an energetic match with success and abundance. We'll start by unearthing the possible core wounds you function from. Don't think. Just write everything that comes to you, even if it's not a whole thought.

Renee Rose

I can't be a millionaire author because

Write to Riches Journal

The lies I'm believing that keep me from being my biggest, brightest self are

Renee Rose

I've been telling myself this lie since...

Write to Riches Journal

The fear or anxiety that makes me stop myself comes from...

I block myself from being the brilliant millionaire author that I am in these ways...

Write to Riches Journal

Are you waiting for someone else to discover you? To give you permission? What are the things you believe must happen before you can go to the next level? Answer the next question with the steps you think have to happen first: (hint, they may not be true. You're just using them as excuses for not having your future life now).

Renee Rose

I will be a successful author when...

Write to Riches Journal

My biggest fear about success is...

Renee Rose

My biggest fear about failure is...

Write to Riches Journal

I distract myself from becoming my future self by...

Renee Rose

My excuses for why I can't move forward yet are...

Addressing your Money Wounds

Let's dig into some of your limiting beliefs around money and wealth. What are your money wounds?

Addressing your Money Wounds

What beliefs do you have about rich people?

Addressing your Money Wounds

What will happen if you get rich?

What do you hate about money?

Addressing your Money Wounds

What do you love about money?

I can't be rich because...

Addressing your Money Wounds

What belief about money or wealth limits you the most?

Addressing your Money Wounds

What will happen if I am seen as the writer I am....

Addressing your Money Wounds

Now that you've mined your subconscious for limiting beliefs and thought patterns, disrupt them using one or more of the clearing methods described in Chapter Three, "How to Clear the Crud".

Clearing Resistance to New Self Image

What judgments are you making about your own life right now? What structures or patterns in your life keep you in the box, doing the same thing over and over again? What beliefs, prejudices, points of view are keeping you small?

Clearing Resistance to New Self Image

How am I making myself small?

Clearing Resistance to New Self Image

$$$

Clearing Resistance to New Self Image

Make a list or fill a page answering this question:
   What are you unwilling to be?

Clearing Resistance to New Self Image

$$$

Clearing Resistance to New Self Image

I'm sure you have very good reasons for not wanting to be all of those things.

Are you willing to clear all of it, so there is no polarity or charge on any of this, and you can create the abundant life you're asking for? Write a giant yes on the line below or affirm it out loud.

Clearing Resistance to New Self Image

After you mine these prompts, what clearing strategy tools will help you clear these from your field? Lean in and do the clearings.

Feeding the Fire and Finding Your Why

The next step to manifesting abundance is feeding the fire. This is where you get clear on your intentions, find your why and pull in the feelings and energy that manifesting those intentions will bring.

This is the fun part! You get to brainstorm your perfect life. Keep in mind this can be an ever-evolving map. You're not locking yourself into anything. You can change your targets midstream. You can choose, then refine that choice, or choose something new over and over again. There are no wrong choices, other than having the belief that there are wrong choices.

If you could wave a magic wand to transform your life or career in any way, what would you wish for?

Feeding the Fire and Finding Your Why

Feeding the Fire and Finding Your Why

Feeding the Fire and Finding Your Why

What does your perfect, magic-wanded life look like?

Feeding the Fire and Finding Your Why

Feeding the Fire and Finding Your Why

Where do you want to be as an author in three years?

Feeding the Fire and Finding Your Why

Feeding the Fire and Finding Your Why

Put yourself there—imagine it's already happened. What does your life look like?

Feeding the Fire and Finding Your Why

Feeding the Fire and Finding Your Why

What are you doing differently? Better?

Feeding the Fire and Finding Your Why

Is that something you can already integrate today?

Feeding the Fire and Finding Your Why

What is one thing you could do immediately that would improve your career?

Feeding the Fire and Finding Your Why

What is one thing you could do today that would improve your quality of life and/or make you feel abundant?

Feeding the Fire and Finding Your Why

What successes and accomplishments you've already had can you honor and celebrate right now?

Feeding the Fire and Finding Your Why

How will you reward yourself for meeting your targets?

Feeding the Fire and Finding Your Why

What are examples of three perfect Millionaire Author days? (Hint–this makes a great morning exercise, to imagine more and more variations on the perfect day.)

For example, you wake up, and your sexy partner has already made you a perfect, foamy cappuccino. Your assistant texts to tell you all the things she's going to do for you today, and that you don't need to worry about a thing from the administrative end–just focus on your wonderful book. You have a long, uninterrupted shower in which all kinds of creative thoughts download and get you excited for the scenes you have to write. You grab your pre-packed beach bag and walk down to the beach (because you live just a few feet away, of course!) where you sit under an umbrella and write, easily and effortlessly getting way more than your planned word count in for the day. Then you head back home where a massage therapist has already set up to give you a wonderful massage. That night, you stop in at your local bookstore, where you have a scheduled signing, and there's a line wrapped around the building, just for you. You soak it all in, smiling and waving, loving your fans who love you in return...

Okay, that has never been mine, but now that I wrote it for you, I might incorporate that into my dream machine!

Feeding the Fire and Finding Your Why

Feeding the Fire and Finding Your Why

Clarifying Your Intentions

Clarifying Your Intentions

Where do you want to be as an author in three years?

Clarifying Your Intentions

Clarifying Your Intentions

Put yourself there—imagine it's already happened. What does your life look like?

Clarifying Your Intentions

What are you doing differently? Better?

Is that something you can already integrate today?

Clarifying Your Intentions

What is one thing you could do immediately that would improve your career?

What's the next step for you in your writing career?

Clarifying Your Intentions

What blocks you from being the brilliant millionaire author that you are?

Clarifying Your Intentions

Love Your Books

In step three, we bring in the love. Loving your books can be the single most powerful tool for creating more in your author business. The more you admire, celebrate and acknowledge how amazing your work is, the more you will flourish.

Look to the places where you judge yourself most, pour some ego sauce on it to flip your limiting beliefs, and uncover how that is actually one of your greatest strengths.

Love Your Books

What are the three (or more) areas I judge myself most?

Love Your Books

Love Your Books

If I pour ego sauce on it, what potential lies in those areas?

Love Your Books

What are the gifts I'm hiding from myself?

Love Your Books

What do I love about my book or books?

Love Your Books

Love Your Books

What do I do well as a writer?

Love Your Books

Love Your Books

What do my books want me to know?

When I ask this question, the hero of my book often talks to me, reassuring me that the book is going to be loved, or I'm shown a scene that's missing.

Love Your Books

Love Your Books

How can I receive more from my books?

You might not get words to write down from this prompt. Rather, it could show up as more of an energetic receiving than anything words can express. Just open up your awareness to whatever comes. Whether it's just a feel-good or the energy of the book, take it in.

Love Your Books

Love Your Books

What am I grateful for in my author career?

Which people are a gift or contribution to my career?

Even just asking this question invites more helpful people into your world.

Meditation: Love your Books

Use this meditation to connect with the energy of your books and surround them with love.

1. Close your eyes. Imagine your energy like a giant ball of light that extends three feet beyond you in every direction.
2. Expand your energy out a hundred million miles to encompass all that is.
3. Invite in the energy of a particular book, series, or your entire catalog.
4. Take a moment to just experience the energy of that book or series of books.
5. Send gratitude to your work. Thank it for being. Love it.
6. Ask it what it needs from you. (Often authors hear that it just needs more love or to be appreciated, but you may get a specific task or marketing idea)
7. Reverse the flow of energy and receive from your work. What does it want to gift to you? How can it contribute to your life? Will you allow it to contribute?

Meditation: Love your Books

8. Repeat steps five and seven, sending gratitude and receiving back from your book as many times as feels good or interesting to you. When you're finished, thank the book or books again before you disconnect from their energy, open your eyes and return to your day.

Meditation: Love your Books

Record any thoughts, impressions, insights from the meditation...

Trust Your Gut

In step four, you learn how to tap into your intuition and use it for all business decisions big or small. This workbook/journal is the perfect tool for receiving guidance and learning to trust your gut.

Think of the times you've trusted your gut (or not followed a gut instinct). What did it feel like? How did you know it was intuition talking and not fear or logic? Play with the following freewriting exercises to help tap into this powerful tool.

Trust Your Gut

Where do you not trust yourself?

Trust Your Gut

Where do you trust yourself?

Trust Your Gut

What intuitive hits have you had in the past?

....
....
....
....
....
....
....
....
....
....

Where have you acted on intuition in your life?

....
....
....
....
....
....
....
....
....

Trust Your Gut

What method or methods of tapping into your inner knowing work best for you?

When and where are you the most open to intuitive hits?

Meditation: Money Pull and Receiving

Often we've created abundance somewhere in the multiverse, but it hasn't shown up in this timeline or in the present. This meditation is wonderful for pulling money into the here and now.

1. Close your eyes and imagine your energy like a ball of light around you.
2. Extend it out to the furthest reaches of the Universe.
3. Make the demand that the amount of money you desire show up now. You could say, "I'll have the money now, please" or even, "I demand the money show up now." Notice how there's a power and potency to demanding versus the energy of begging for money.
4. Open up to receive the abundance, allowing it to flow into your energy field and stay. You might picture it like a snowstorm of hundred dollar bills that swirl around you from all sides and stick to you like glue.
5. Feel the gratitude that accompanies that abundance–how the vibrations are the same. Turn up that sensation of gratitude. Revel in it for as long as you like.

Meditation: Money Pull and Receiving

6. Thank the Universe (or whoever you want to thank) for the abundance that is on its way to you.

Meditation: Money Pull and Receiving

Record any thoughts, impressions, insights from the meditation...

Live it Now

In step five we pull in the energy of the future we wish to create and act as if we already have everything we desire. It's the "fake it until you make it" except you won't be faking the energy—that part has to be real. In order to be a millionaire author, you have to act and think like one. Treat yourself like one.

Where are the places you deny yourself? What do you desire that evokes the feeling of abundance in you?

Live it Now

How can I immerse myself in luxury today? (Is it getting 1000 thread count Egyptian cotton sheets for your bed? Is it buying a feather pillow?)

Live it Now

What can I choose to be my Millionaire Author token or symbol, and what is the energy it embodies?

Live it Now

What am I denying myself that if I would indulge would make me feel rich?

Live it Now

Where could I have more possibilities and ease in my life?

Meditation: Hot Tub Time Machine

In the Author Abundance monthly membership, I led a "Hot Tub Time Machine" meditation in which you travel to meet your future self–the one who has already achieved everything you seek to achieve.

1. Close your eyes and imagine you are entering the most luxurious hot tub. Maybe it's the kind with a waterfall. Maybe it's filled with salt water.
2. You step into the hot tub, and it transports you to another time or dimension. One in which you already are the successful, *New York Times* Bestselling Millionaire author, or whatever it is you're striving for.
3. Climb out of the hot tub and stand face to face with your alternate self. You may want to reach out and hold her hands, or look into her eyes.
4. Check in–what does she want you to know? What message does she have for you? What advice?
5. Synchronize your energy with hers.

Meditation: Hot Tub Time Machine

6. Open up to receive any encouragement, love, or gratitude from her.
7. Thank her and return to the hot tub to transport you back to the current time-space reality.
8. Open your eyes and go out into your day with the gifts or information you received from your alternate self.

Record any thoughts, impressions, insights from the meditation...

Meditation: Hot Tub Time Machine

Embodying Your Future Self

Be Vigilant with your Word. Where do I want to be as an author in five years?

Put yourself there—imagine it's already happened. What does my life look like?

Embodying Your Future Self

Embodying Your Future Self

Embodying Your Future Self

What am I doing differently? Better?

Embodying Your Future Self

Is it something I can already integrate today? How?

Embodying Your Future Self

What is one thing I could do immediately that would improve my lifestyle?

What is one thing I could do immediately that would improve my career?

Embodying Your Future Self

What's the next step for me in my writing career?

Embodying Your Future Self

Embodying Your Future Self

What blocks me from being the brilliant millionaire author that I am? Imagine that block, and recast it, reenvision it, rewrite it.

Embodying Your Future Self

Let it Be

Step six is to let it be.

Take the pressure off achieving your goals by pretending it's already happened (as in Step 5, Live it Now). Trusting it's on its way to you.

Sometimes the best thing you can do for your career or your future is to get out of your own way. You sent your request out to the Universe, now give it time and space to gel. Open up to receive without trying to control the outcome.

Let it Be

What areas of my career and life am I trying to control that if I'd just let go would finally bloom?

Let it Be

Let it Be

What decisions have I made about the things I need to do or the order they need to happen that may be limiting my possibilities?

Let it Be

Let it Be

How have I decided success can happen for me? Are there other ways it might happen?

Let it Be

What infinite possibilities are available for my books? My career?

Let it Be

Let it Be

Where do I allow for the magic of the Universe in my life?

Let it Be

Imagine that you have surrendered to the magic of the Universe. Feel into that. What does it feel like? Explore that place of freedom.

Let it Be

Hit the Easy Button

Use the freewriting prompts below to discover where you're trying to get it right or afraid of getting it wrong. Can you leave both of these behind and go back to the simplicity of the third step to author abundance—*love your books*? That's the energy you want to be in. Nothing to prove. Nothing to fear. You don't have to have all the answers. They will show up at the exact time you require them.

Hit the Easy Button

Where am I trying to "get it right?" / What am I afraid of getting "wrong?"

Hit the Easy Button

Hit the Easy Button

What am I trying to prove? Who am I trying to prove it to?

Hit the Easy Button

Where have I been conditioned to do or be or believe something?

Hit the Easy Button

Hit the Easy Button

What have I already tried and "failed" that I've decided I will never do again?

Hit the Easy Button

What do I believe will never work for me?

Hit the Easy Button

What limiting decisions have I made or conditions set like If I have _____ then _____.

Hit the Easy Button

Where do I limit myself? What infinite possibilities are available in this situation?

Hit the Easy Button

Hit the Easy Button

Think about something that's going on in your life right now that you'd like to turn over to the Universe. With love in your heart and that situation in your consciousness, ask: what else is possible over and over again. Just allowing for possibilities to show up.

Hit the Easy Button

Hit the Easy Button

Honor Yourself

Step seven is about honoring yourself first and foremost. This is where you make sure you are nurturing yourself, setting appropriate boundaries, and taking care of your body.

Ask your body what it wants to eat before your next meal and trust whatever shows up in your mind. If you're at a restaurant, try asking your body first, then scanning the menu to see where your eye is drawn.

Check in with your body and write the first response that comes to mind on each of the following questions:

What kind of movement does my body want to do today?

Honor Yourself

Is there something special my body requires (massage, acupuncture, a doctor visit, a spa visit, etc)

Tune in and ask your body where it wants to work today.

Honor Yourself

Ask your body if it likes the space you call your office. If no, ask it what it would like. Maybe it wants a new paint color or to rearrange the furniture.

Abundance Meditation: Energy Alignment

1. Close your eyes.
2. Perceive your energy bubble around you, about three feet in all directions.
3. Now expand the energy field until it's as big as the room you're in.
4. Expand it until it's as big as the block you're on. As big as the city you're in. As big as the state or province. As big as the country you're in. Expand until you're as big as the Earth. Now as big as the galaxy. Expand your energy field out a hundred million miles in every direction.
5. Open to receive all the possibilities, all the gifts of the Universe. Invite in the energy of *USA Today Bestseller* for the book of your choice. If this is a target you've already hit, invite in the energy of being number one on the list, or staying there for twenty weeks, or having five books on the list at once—whatever feels fun to you!
6. Ask that energy to come into your field. Invite it into your body, into every cell. Ask it to sync up with your energy field. Look for any place the energy won't sync up—

Abundance Meditation: Energy Alignment

anything that doesn't allow this energy to be yours and ask it to come into harmony or leave.

If you're already geared up to make a list run for a particular book, ask your book what it requires from you, either energetically or in actuality.

Abundance Meditation: Energy Alignment

Record any thoughts, impressions, insights from the meditation...

Celebrate to Create

The energy of gratitude is almost the same as abundance, which is why *every manifesting process includes gratitude.*

The more you celebrate every win, the everyday ones like writing a thousand words, figuring out the next piece of your plot, sending out your newsletter, the more easily things will flow for you. Pat yourself on the back a hundred times today and watch how you start to create everything with total ease.

Celebrate to Create

List five wins you can celebrate that you accomplished in the last week. They can be small wins or big wins. The more you acknowledge, the easier things get. It's like lubricating the wheels to success.

Celebrate to Create

Celebrate to Create

What successes and accomplishments have you already had that you can honor and celebrate right now?

....
....
....
....
....
....
....
....
....
....
....
....
....
....
....
....
....
....
....
....
....
....
....

Celebrate to Create

Celebrate to Create

How will you reward yourself for meeting your targets?

Celebrate to Create

How can you improve as a writer?

Celebrate to Create

What did you create in the past year you'd like to acknowledge?

What was awesome, amazing, and what did you follow through on?

Celebrate to Create

What did you target, go for, and actualize?

Celebrate to Create

What showed up that surprised and delighted you, magically?

Stop Judging Yourself

Stop looking for all the answers outside of yourself. Be open to your answers showing up. Yes, they might show up through an expert's opinion or teaching on a certain topic, some inspiration you get from something you see, but you're ultimately the one who knows whether their method will work for you or not or how you're going to use it. You'll know if you get excited about it. If it feels fun and easy. If implementing it flows smoothly.

Stop Judging Yourself

Where (and when and with whom) are you not honoring your time / honoring yourself?

Stop Judging Yourself

Where (and when) are you judging yourself, being hard on yourself, or not valuing yourself?

Stop Judging Yourself

Where (and about what) do you put high expectations on yourself that are not possible or that you weren't going to do anyway?

Stop Judging Yourself

When did you expect yourself to meet linear requirements or perform in a prescribed way in order to fulfill your targets? Could you hit your targets in a new and different way?

Stop Judging Yourself

Stop Judging Yourself

Is there anything you feel shameful about? Would you be willing to clear the judgment around it? Forgive yourself? (See Step One for clearing methods).

Stop Judging Yourself

Where are you doubting your own knowing and trying to follow the experts' advice?

Stop Judging Yourself

Where are you trying to fix yourself instead of acknowledging how great you already are?

Stop Judging Yourself

Where are you resisting your own greatness?

Be Gentle With Yourself

When we give ourselves grace, when we are gentle and kind and nurturing during the times we believe we're not measuring up, it's easy to move through the tougher times and get back on track. Not only back on track—to rocket forward.

Be Gentle With Yourself

What are all the ways I could receive help?

Be Gentle With Yourself

Who or what are part of my energetic team?

Be Gentle With Yourself

How can I open to receive more from them?

Abundance Meditation: Attracting Reviews

Only you can shape how that energy affects your book. Hint—it's not through the words of the review, it's through your reaction (or non-reaction) to them.

Want to energize your book with reviews?

1. Close your eyes and drop your barriers.
2. Expand your energy out until it's as big as the room you're in. Then as big as your block. Then as big as your city. As big as your state or province. Expand out to fill the space of your entire country. Now the Earth. Now the galaxy. And finally, the Universe.
3. Hold your book in your hands with your imagination or with your physical book—your choice—they both work the same!
4. Imagine a magnet on your book that draws all the amazing reviews it could possibly receive.

Abundance Meditation: Attracting Reviews

5. Then drop away any point of view about good or bad reviews and just receive the energy of all reviews, tons of eyes and opinions on your book.
6. Feel the energy around your book growing and growing with the more energetic reviews you receive.
7. Send gratitude back out to all the reviews for energizing your book.

Abundance Meditation: Attracting Reviews

Record any thoughts, impressions, insights from the meditation...

Additional Pages

Additional Pages

Tapping into my genius...

Additional Pages

Tapping into my genius...

Additional Pages

Tapping into my genius...

Additional Pages

Tapping into my genius...

Additional Pages

Tapping into my genius...

Additional Pages

Tapping into my genius...

Additional Pages

Tapping into my genius...

Additional Pages

Tapping into my genius...

Additional Pages

Tapping into my genius...

Additional Pages

Tapping into my genius...

Additional Pages

Tapping into my genius...

Additional Pages

Tapping into my genius...

Additional Pages

Tapping into my genius...

Additional Pages

Tapping into my genius...

Additional Pages

Tapping into my genius...

Additional Pages

Tapping into my genius...

Additional Pages

Tapping into my genius...

Additional Pages

Tapping into my genius...

Additional Pages

Tapping into my genius...

Additional Pages

Tapping into my genius...

Additional Pages

Tapping into my genius...

Additional Pages

Tapping into my genius...

Additional Pages

Tapping into my genius...

Additional Pages

Tapping into my genius...

Additional Pages

Tapping into my genius...

Additional Pages

Tapping into my genius...

Additional Pages

Tapping into my genius...

Additional Pages

Tapping into my genius...

Additional Pages

Tapping into my genius...

Additional Pages

Tapping into my genius...

Additional Pages

Tapping into my genius...

About Renee Rose

15-time **USA Today bestselling romance author Renee Rose** is passionate about helping other authors find and maintain an abundance mindset to catapult their careers and create their best future. She employs energetic tools and techniques to help her clients clear resistance and money blocks, access their inner guidance, and tap into their love and appreciation for their books so they can achieve their dreams.

www.write2riches.com
renee@reneeroseromance.com

facebook.com/reneeroseromance
instagram.com/writetoriches
amazon.com/Renee-Rose/e/B008AS0FT0
bookbub.com/authors/renee-rose
tiktok.com/@write2riches

www.ingramcontent.com/pod-product-compliance
Lightning Source LLC
Chambersburg PA
CBHW072003070526
44583CB00015B/1310